Inclu... ...o are
Work... ...els

Written by
Janet Beckett and Kay Holman

Illustrated by
Martha Hardy

Published 2010 by A&C Black Publishers Limited
36 Soho Square, London W1D 3QY
www.acblack.com

ISBN 978-1-4081-295-17

First published in the UK, 2006 (Updated 2007)

Text © Janet Beckett & Kay Holman, 2006
Illustrations © Martha Hardy

Printed in Great Britain by Latimer Trend & Company Limited

This book is produced using paper that is made from wood grown in
managed, sustainable forests. It is natural, renewable and recyclable.
The logging and manufacturing processes conform to the environmental
regulations of the country of origin.

**To see our full range of titles
visit www.acblack.com**

Contents

Introduction

This book has been written to help you:

- to engage children who are difficult to engage
- to identify individual needs
- to plan a 'small steps' approach
- to understand and plan for children who may be working at stages not easily identified within the EYFS Early Learning Goals or National Curriculum Levels.

About the the P scales

Many children with additional needs make very small steps in their learning and may make these steps unevenly, or only gradually, over a long time. Practitioners, teachers and parents wanted to recognise progress within these small steps and found that the EYFS framework and the National Curriculum Levels were not describing the small steps in sufficient detail. In response to this need, the Qualifications and Curriculum Authority (QCA) developed the P scales to be used as assessment criteria to measure progress below Level 1 in the National Curriculum Programmes of Study.

> **The P scales were written to define progress for pupils of statutory school age (5-16)**

It is very important to remember that the P levels and scales are intended for use within and beyond Key Stage 1. Practitioners and settings should be cautious about using the P scales to assess children at earlier stages:

"The P scales are assessment criteria for progress below Level one in the national curriculum programmes of study. These programmes are designed for pupils aged 5-16. They were developed to support target setting through the use of summative assessment to be used at the end of key stages and, for those pupils making more rapid progress, possibly once a year." QCA

More information about the P scales can be obtained from the DCSF (Department for Children, Schools and Families) and the QCA (Qualifications and Curriculum Authority):

Since they were first developed, the P scales have been updated:

The P scales that can be accessed from the QCA website **www.qca.org.uk** replace the version of the P scales previously included in 'Supporting the Target Setting Process' (now out of print) and discussed in 'Planning, Teaching and Assessing the Curriculum for Pupils with Learning Difficulties' (this is available as a download from the QCA website). This revision was carried out in 2004, when the P scales for English, mathematics, science and ICT were revised. The revised P scales for these subjects supersede those published in 2001 and can be found at **www.qca.org.uk.**

"QCA, in conjunction with the DCSF, has made minor revisions to the P scales. Practitioners requested more age-appropriate examples for secondary pupils, more up-to-date examples of ICT and some clarification of the level descriptors from P4 to P8.

We have:

- separated the speaking and listening strands in English.

- reviewed the descriptions between levels P4 to level 1 of the national curriculum in English, mathematics, ICT and science."

Materials available from QCA

'Planning, teaching and assessing the curriculum for pupils with learning difficulties':
QCA guidance on the national curriculum for all those who work with pupils with learning difficulties.

'Supporting school improvement: emotional and behavioural development':
Guidance on setting improvement targets for pupils (available from QCA publications for £3; downloadable from the QCA page).

'Data collection and the analysis of P scale assessment data':
QCA organises annual data collection and the analysis of P scale assessment data in order to establish a national picture of the performance of pupils working significantly below age-related expectations and to prepare analyses from the resulting dataset to support school self-evaluation and the setting of school improvement targets.

'Shared world: different experiences':
Guidance on planning, teaching and evaluating a curriculum that will help pupils who are deaf and blind make progress in a range of settings (available from QCA publications – £6).

The relationship between the P Scales and the Early Learning Goals

'The Early Learning Goals specify expectations for children's progression by the end of the Foundation Stage, while the P scales were written for use with children of national curriculum age who are working towards level 1 or who are working within levels 1 or 2 of the national curriculum for extended periods of time. They were written primarily for supporting target setting in the context of the National Curriculum.

The Early Learning Goals themselves (and consequently items 4–8 in any ESP scale) are not necessarily hierarchical and do not necessarily reflect progression.'

You can download and print the P Scales from the QCA website **www.qca.org.uk**. They provide interesting and useful reference points when looking at the very early stages of learning, and for older children are a general indication of the current stage of development of a child with additional needs.

> **The P scales were written to define progress for pupils of statutory school age (5-16)**

There are P scales for:

- English (3 scales; Reading; Writing; Speaking and Listening)
- Mathematics (3 scales: Shape, Space and Measures; Number; Using and Applying Mathematics)
- Science
- ICT

Each scale contains eight P Scale descriptions and a transition to Level 1 of the National Curriculum. Levels P1 to P3 in each scale show the earliest levels of general attainment and are common across all subjects. Levels P4 to P8 show subject-related attainment. Here is a sample from Speaking and Listening:

Listening/Receptive Communication Descriptor	
P1(i) Pupils encounter activities and experiences. They may be passive or resistant. They may show simple reflex responses, for example, startling at sudden noises or movements. Any participation is fully prompted.	No additional guidance for this scale point
P1(ii) Pupils show emerging awareness of activities and experiences. They may have periods when they appear alert and ready to focus their attention on certain people, events, objects or parts of objects, for example, attending briefly to interactions with a familiar person. They may give intermittent reactions, for example, sometimes becoming excited in the midst of social activity.	No additional guidance for this scale point **Use these statements with caution when working with under fives!**

Some scale descriptions include additional guidance on the characteristics and expectations of a child at that level, most do not.

A word of caution!

QCA and the DCSF suggest:

- that P Scales should only be used to measure the attainment or progress of children once they have a statement of Special Educational Need.

- that P Scales should be used with caution with children who have not yet reached Statutory School Age (i.e. the term after their fifth birthday).

The P scales are **not** designed to be used:

- as a crude performance indicator for making staff or schools accountable for effectiveness

- for detailed formative assessment

- to define curriculum content or as a detailed step-by-step curriculum

- to assess progress outside the 5–16 age range

- as labels to describe pupils

- for diagnosing or identifying pupils' special educational needs

- as targets for individual pupils. The broad, subject-focused nature of the P scale level descriptors means that they do not make good short-term targets for addressing the individual needs of particular pupils.

Flo Longhorn in her series of books about very special people (**www.amazon.co.uk**) describes the way pupils may experience the world. She describes how pupils:

- encounter by being present during an experience

- become aware by noticing that something is going on

- begin to respond by showing surprise, enjoyment or dissatisfaction

- engage by directing attention, focusing their looking or listening, they may show interest, recognition or recall

- participate by sharing, turn taking, anticipating and through supported involvement

- become involved through active participation, reaching out, joining in, doing and commenting

- achieve by consolidating and practising skills, knowledge, concepts and understanding.

This series of processes, although it is not necessarily presented in the order that we see in individual children, should help when recognising responses made by children with additional needs.

How practitioners might use the P scales

Before you start:

- Confirm that the child really does have special or additional needs. Some children have delayed development, but this is still within the normal range and just needs you to give more time, support or additional materials. These children have additional needs, but their needs can be met within your regular planning.

  However, some children may already have a statement or be in the process of being assessed for a statement of Special Educational Need. Other professionals may already be involved in supporting the child and their family, and you will know very soon that the range of differentiation you usually offer is not going to be enough.

> **How can I use the P scale statements to help with planning for individual needs?**

- Have a look at the P Scale statements and see if they can help you to recognise the child's abilities and needs. Do they behave and react in the ways described in the statements? Could the statements help you to plan activities that meet their needs more closely? Do they help you to notice what the child **can** do, rather than what they can't? Do they help you to realise that there are many small steps in a child's learning?

- Get a mental map of the statements in your head. You may not need to use the statements to plan, just as a nudge to your thinking as you plan for the day.

> **How could I use the ideas in this book?**

Once you have considered these aspects, look at the activities in the second part of this book and think whether they might be relevant to children in your group, and how you might use them:

- Use some of the ideas in this book to help you plan for individual activities which link to P Scale statements.

- Use the ideas for the whole group, and use the P Scale statements to help you look, listen and reflect on what all the children are doing and achieving.

- Use your own ideas, then map the experiences onto the P Scale statements.

Remember, this book has been written by two early years practitioners and your ideas may be just as good as theirs!

Some additional resources

Like many other practitioners working with children with additional needs, the writers of this book have taken their understanding of the child working within the early P levels from a variety of sources. Not least of these is their personal experience of teaching in a school for pupils with severe, profound and multiple learning difficulties. They have researched and used the QCA P scales which give descriptors of what can be expected of children at the very earliest levels.

The original P scales have been developed and expanded by three organisations: Lancashire County Council in their PIVATS document, B Squared and Equals.

Visit these websites for more information

PIVATS is described on the website for Lancashire Local Authority (LA) – **www.lancashire.gov.uk** – as:

- performance Indicators for Value Added Target Setting (PIVATS) is based up on the revised performance criteria published by DfES and QCA (2001) in 'Supporting the Target Setting Process – Guidance for Effective Target Setting for Pupils with Special Educational Needs'

- A system to inform target setting for pupils of all ages whose performance is outside national expectations.

- A system to complement and work alongside statutory assessment at Foundation Stage and Key Stages 1, 2, 3 and 4.

- An approach that may be used annually, as a baseline assessment or as a yearly measurement of added value.

BSquared www.bsquaredsen.co.uk have also developed software and paper versions of early learning records linked to the EYFS Curriculum.

Their early Steps Summative Assessment is based on the Foundation document and covers Physical development (PD), Communication, language and literacy (CLL), Problem solving reasoning and numeracy (PSRN), Knowledge of the World (KUW) and Creative development (CD).

Equals www.equals.co.uk also produce materials to support practitioners in using the P scales:

"The new PACE2 document includes new assessment tasks with reference to all of the new P scales. It has also increased the number of items to be assessed in every P level. The new document will be required by all of those who wish to enter data into the EQUALS Target Setting Project in 2005."

The PACE2 document is:

- a tool to support curriculum development, school improvement and self-evaluation

- a common structure and language for schools and services to judge pupil performance

- fundamental to the inclusion of all pupils

- linked to the National Curriculum average point score

- the performance criteria have become known as the P scales.

Helping parents to understand their child's additional needs.

Here are the thoughts and feelings of one mother as her son started school at four years old:

We will be celebrating Daniel's 4th birthday this month. The following story was sent to me by a friend, two years after I had Daniel, when I was still really angry and asking, 'Why?'.

"When you're going to have a baby it's like planning a fabulous holiday to Italy. You buy all the guidebooks and make your wonderful plans; the Coliseum, the Michelangelo David, the gondolas in Venice. You learn some handy Italian phrases and you're very excited. After months of eager anticipation the day finally arrives. You pack your bags and off you go. Several hours later the plane lands.

The flight attendant comes and says 'Welcome to Holland'. 'HOLLAND?! You say, what do you mean Holland? I signed up for Italy! All my life I've dreamed of going to Italy!' 'But there has been a change in the flight plan, we have landed in Holland and this is where you have to stay,' says the attendant.

The important thing is they haven't taken you to a horrible, disgusting, filthy place full of pestilence, famine and disease. It is just a different place. So, you go and buy new guide books, you learn a whole new language and you prepare to meet a whole new group of people you would never have met. It's just a different place, it's slower paced than Italy, less flashy than Italy. After you have been there for a while you catch your breath, you look around, and you begin to see how nice Holland is with its windmills, tulips and Rembrandts. However, when you get home, everyone you know is coming and going from Italy and they all brag about what a wonderful time they had there. For the rest of your life you will say, 'Yes, that's where I was supposed to go, that is what I had planned, and the pain of that means I will never, ever, ever go away again because of the loss of that dream'. But if you spend your life mourning the fact that you didn't get to Italy, you may never be free to enjoy the very special, the very lovely things about Holland."

During my pregnancy I prayed to God a lot about my unborn child and told him I would love the child no matter what – all that I asked in return was that he would give me a child I could love and that the child would love me. God answered my prayer in Daniel who is, without a doubt, the most loving, beautiful and happy child I have ever known. Even in the dark days I never stopped loving him (how could anyone not warm to him) but I did cry and say I wouldn't have had him if I'd known how many problems we were up against. For nearly two years he didn't appear to recognise us, all the effort I put in and he didn't even know I was his mummy! As time has passed he continues to make amazing progress even in the face of all the set backs. He brings so much pleasure to everyone who has dealings with him and that makes me proud. I believe we have learnt to enjoy him as he is and can't imagine him any other way. I wouldn't change Daniel for the world, he is my little Star – and 'HOLLAND' does not seem so bad after all!

Rosalind Oldham; July 2005

Planning for children with identified special needs

Planning for Daniel and children like him, whose parents love them despite their needs, syndromes and problems, will be a challenge. Practitioners must take hold of that challenge, ensuring that all children in their setting have equal access to the curriculum and the whole range of activities described in EYFS practice guidance, cards and disk.

Of course, you will have to adapt activities in different ways:

- Some children may need the activity repeated many times.

- Some may need to sit or lie down near activities that other children access standing up.

- Some may need you to help them by showing what to do – modelling even the simplest of activities, of helping them to grip or hold equipment.

- Some may need adapted resources, such as thicker handles on brushes, special scissors, bigger containers for glue and paint, more substantial protective clothing.

- Some may need help or care when out of doors, because they get cold more quickly, need to be physically moved from activity to activity, or need adapted equipment and toys.

- Some may need individual activities, their own tray of sand, piece of dough, bowl of water, because they can't manage in a group.

- Some may need much longer, or much shorter periods of activity, so you need to be more flexible and responsive.

- Some may get tired easily and need you to arrange rest and recuperation at frequent intervals.

And they will all need you to watch, listen and note what happens, so you can be:

- flexible; adapting activities as you go

- responsive; giving help when needed, but not rushing in too soon

- appreciative; giving praise and reward for effort and achievement

- reflective; feeding back what they do as a reinforcement

- forward thinking; noticing and planning for the next steps in learning

- open; noticing, recognising and appreciating other aspects of learning and skills, some of which you may not have planned for or be expecting.

Introduction to the activity pages

In the following pages you will find some examples of activities which are planned to meet the needs of children who are working well below the expected levels for their age. When using these ideas to help you in your work, remember the following ten tips:

This page contains ten tips for success

Ten Tips for Success

1. Always observe the child carefully before assuming that you can use the activity without modifying it.

2. Start at the beginning – it's better to start at a simpler level, so the child experiences success. You can always make the activity more challenging when you present it the next time.

3. Preparation is the key to success! Always read the instructions carefully before you start, collect all the resources you need and have everything prepared. The child you are working with may not be able to concentrate for long, and you may miss the 'window of opportunity' if you have to leave to fetch something you have forgotten.

4. Watch carefully as you work and play alongside the child. Then you will know whether to go on, to stop, to make it more challenging or to give more help.

5. Praise and positive feedback are so important – make sure you praise all effort, not just outcomes. Use reinforcement and positive feedback as you praise – 'Good listening!' 'Great holding!' 'You smiled then, did you enjoy that?' 'Do you want to do it again?'

6. Don't go on too long! Some children have **very** short attention spans, and need little and often. Stop when they are tired or lose concentration, and return to the activity later or another day. Don't feel that more is necessarily better.

7. Take photos as you go – much of the learning will be fleeting, and you will need to record significant achievements, movements or expressions.

8. Watch, listen and reflect on what you see. Try to be objective.

9. Be patient – you may have to repeat things over and over again before you see any improvement.

10. Encourage independence – don't be tempted to do things for a child, be patient and give them time to do things for themselves.

Key to the activity pages

Please read the following key before using the activities:

What does this activity help with?

This will tell you which skill or area of learning the activity will help with.

Suitable for:

The group size – one-to-one or a small group.

What you need:

This box gives guidance on what you need for the main activity. Extension or follow-up activities may need additional resources.

Always check!

Relevant P scale statements

In this box you will find some of the relevant P scale statements.
These are usually from P1 to P3 for Communication. Some are from the P scales for Mathematics or ICT.

What you do:

Simple instructions for the main activity. You may have to adjust these according to the needs of individuals or groups.

You may also decide not to complete the whole activity if it is obviously too long, too difficult or the child is tired or has lost interest.

Some more ideas:

These are extensions or alternatives to add to the original idea. You may want to use these in later sessions or as alternatives to the main idea.

Watch, listen and reflect:

Tips for observation and assessment.

Activity Two
Smile please

What does this activity help with?

Developing self care routines.

Suitable for: 1:1

What you need:

- small toothbrush

- a variety of flavours of toothpaste

- finger toothbrushes

- glycerine swabs

What you do:

1. Decide where this routine is going to take place and work in the same place each time e.g. in the bathroom.

2. Familiarise the child with the toothbrush by letting them explore it or using it to gently brush their hands and arms.

3. Help the child to become familiar with items in their mouth – you can purchase either finger toothbrushes (latex) or glycerine swab sticks in blackcurrant or lemon.

4. Gradually begin to brush the child's teeth with a small damp brush.

5. Add a small taste of children's toothpaste to the brush.

Some more ideas:

- Try different flavours of toothpaste.

- Try an electric toothbrush.

- Make the activity more fun – add a simple song to the routine such as 'This is the Way We Clean Our Teeth' or 'The Red Toothbrush Goes Up and Down, Up and Down, Up and Down'.

- Talk to your speech and language therapist, who may have more ideas to try.

Relevant P scale statements for Communication

P1 Pupil interacts with people turning to voices looking and smiling at familiar adults.

P2 Pupil makes sounds or gestures to express simple wants or feelings.

P3 Pupil communicates using different sounds/gestures to indicate their likes and dislikes.

Watch, listen and reflect:

How does the child show their likes or dislikes of this routine?

- Does the child tolerate items in their mouth?

- Do they show a preference for particular flavours or colours?

- Does the child begin to anticipate the routine when taken to the bathroom?

Activity Three
Say cheese

What does this activity help with?
Self esteem, feeling a valued and important member of the group.

Suitable for: 1:1

What you need:

- a simple digital camera with a large LCD screen

What you do:

1. This activity is suitable for a child who may not be able to participate in an event in the same way as his/her peers e.g. on Sports Day or during a visit.

2. Use a simple digital camera with a large LCD screen and give the child the important job of being the class or family photographer.

3. Tell the child how important their role is and help them to find good places to take photos from – the finish line at sports day, at the front in assembly, by being first off the bus on a trip.

4. Talk the child through the process, reminding them of what is happening and what they need to do.

5. Make sure you print, discuss and display the photos later with the photographer and with the whole group. Make an album.

Some more ideas:

- You may need to take some extra photos with another camera to make sure you get enough coverage of the event.

- Use a specially adapted camera with a switch mechanism, or invest in a tough camera specially made for children to use (Fisher Price sell a two handed digital with a wide, 'both eyes' viewing screen).

- Talk about and explore the 'delete' button so you can delete photos the child doesn't like. Make sure you explain first that they can't change their mind!

Relevant P scale statements for Communication

P1   Pupil pays attention to surroundings, smiles and turns towards the action.

P2(ii) Pupil reaches for and holds the camera. Pupil may make sounds and gestures in response to cheering.

P3(ii) Pupil holds the camera and may take photos with help. They may respond to familiar people e.g. if the person in the photo is a class member.

Watch, listen and reflect:

How does the child show their enjoyment and sense of pride?

- Does the child smile and enjoy the role?

- Did you make the child feel special and important?

- Does the child become more animated when taking the pictures?

- Can you tell if the child is proud of him/her self? How?

Activity Four
Wow! What good work!

What does this activity help with?

Raises self awareness and self esteem by recognising effort and achievement.

Suitable for: 1:1

What you need:

- no special preparation, just the wide variety of different enjoyable activities available in your setting

What you do:

1. Set up activities that the child really enjoys doing.

2. You may need to try a wide range of activities at different times and using varied equipment.
   Children often respond in different ways on different occasions and at different times. Keep your expectations flexible and responsive to their emerging needs and interests. Don't expect the same response to the same activity!

3. When you have found activities that the child enjoys, join them as they play and celebrate with them. Tell them they have worked well, cheer, clap, and ensure that they know you are pleased.

4. Make sure you celebrate the achievements of all children in the group at group times as well as in individual conversations.

Some more ideas:

- Activities can be simple or complex, easy or challenging, indoors or out.

- Don't just praise activities with an end product, praise such things as playing a game, concentrating during a story, turning the pages in a book, maintaining eye contact.

- Remember to give relevant praise and relate it to a real action – 'Good pointing!' 'You listened really well!' 'Great biking!' 'That's a great puzzle!'

Relevant P scale statements for Communication and ICT

P1 (S & L) Pupil stills in response to a sound. Pupil accepts and is comforted by appropriate physical contact.

P2 (S & L) Pupil makes sounds or gestures to express simple feelings.

P3 (S & L) Pupil communicates using different sounds/gestures to indicate their likes and dislikes.

P6 (ICT) Pupils operate some devices independently.

Watch, listen and reflect:

How does the child show their likes or dislikes of activities and your responses?

- Does the child become more animated?

- Does the child become still?

- Does the child respond to looking at themselves?

- Do they make sounds, gestures, expressions?

Activity Five
Bang the drum

What does this activity help with?

Developing skills of listening, concentration and anticipation.

Suitable for: 1:1

What you need:

- a large drum

What you do:

1. Sit opposite the child with the drum between you.

2. Say or sing this rhyme while beating the drum:
   'Bang the drum, bang the drum
   Name is going to bang the drum
   Bang the drum, bang the drum
   Until it's time tooooooo .... STOP!'

   (You can sing this to the tune of 'Little Brown Jug').

3. Give a drum roll on the words 'time to' getting louder and slower until you say 'STOP'.

4. Now give the child a turn at playing, with you responding to 'STOP'.

5. Encourage the child to anticipate stopping.

6. Repeat the activity if the child indicates (by looking at you, reaching, pointing or vocalising) that they would like more.

Some more ideas:

- Use two smaller drums and copy each other, taking turns to lead and follow.

- Play the game with other instruments – shaking bells, tapping sticks, shaking a tambourine etc.

- Accompany simple songs with percussion instruments, involving other children in the fun.

- Use clapping instead for a simple activity to fill a few minutes.

Relevant P scale statements for Communication

P1 Pupil shows a simple reflex response e.g. is startled by a sudden noise.

P2 Pupil begins to imitate actions such as banging the drum.

P3 Pupil is able to make choices and will request preferred activity by vocalising or pointing to a preferred object.

Watch, listen and reflect:

How does the child show their likes or dislikes of these stop/start games?

- Does the child anticipate the end of the rhyme?

- How does the child indicate they want to play again?

Try leaving a long pause to see if the child will say or indicate 'stop'.

Activity Six
I don't like it!

What does this activity help with?

Helping children to express their likes and dislikes.

Suitable for: 1:

Feathers & Grasses

What you need:

- a wide variety of different resources, aimed at stimulating the senses, and which you think may cause a response. These could include:

    o   Objects to touch – 'koosh' and tactile balls, feathers, tactile fabrics, gloop, slime, dough, jelly etc.

    o   Objects to smell – fruit, perfumed dough, 'smell bottles', flowers etc.

    o   Sound makers – bells, shakers, rain sticks etc.

    o   Objects to see – shiny baubles, foils, mirrors, strongly coloured objects and those with strong patterns.

    o   Things to taste – foods and drinks with strong flavours.

What you do:

1. Focus on one sense at a time.

2. Set up some activities or experiences that you think will provoke a strong response of either like or dislike (this may involve a bit of trial and error!).

3. You may need to try a wide range of activities appealing to the senses. Children often respond differently from our expectations.

4. You will probably need to repeat an activity several times to gain an accurate understanding of the child's response.

5. Observe the child and their responses closely so you don't miss or misinterpret their responses.

6. Make a note of the experiences or objects that they particularly like, and any they really dislike. Particular textures, colours, patterns and smells may trigger extreme responses.

Some more ideas:

- Listen to different types of music at different volumes – classical, rock, folk, dance.

- Listen to different sounds – a loud hooter, soft ringing bells.

- Stroking on different parts of the body with different textures – a feather, chamois leather, cold chains or scouring pads.

- Taste different flavours – sweet, sour, salty or bitter.

- Try different smells: floral, herbal, coffee, chocolate, strong cheese.

Relevant P scale statements for Communication

P1 Pupil may be passive or resistant to a range of sensory stimuli.

P2 Pupil makes sounds, gestures or other responses to express simple wants or feelings.

P3 Pupil communicates simple choices, likes or dislikes.

Watch, listen and reflect:

How does the child show their likes or dislikes of these experiences?

- Do they become still?

- Do mouth movements increase?

- Does the child become more animated?

- Does the child 'close down' and feign sleep?

Activity Seven
Let rip

What does this activity help with?

The development of awareness of sound.

Suitable for: 1:1 or a small group

What you need:

- a box of different sorts of paper – tissue, thin card, greaseproof, foil, wrapping

What you do:

1. Use a puppet to make different sounds with a large piece of paper e.g. shaking, waving, tapping, scrunching, and ripping the paper.

2. Encourage the pupils to imitate the sounds with a piece of paper of their own. They may need help.

3. Sing the song 'Everybody do this' as the puppet accompanies the song with a paper sound and the pupils join in.

4. Repeat with different sorts of paper, newspaper, tissue, thin card, greaseproof, wrapping paper, foil etc.

5. The puppet hands out 1 piece of paper to a child, singing: 'Charlie's turn to do this, do this, do this, Charlie's turn to do this just like me'. Charlie makes sound with paper.

6. If they are ready for more, sing the song with new words and the child doing the actions, such as 'This is how you tear it...' etc.

Some more ideas:

- Explore some of these: crinkly paper, corrugated paper, bubble wrap, sandpaper, Velcro, zips, strings of pasta, bottle tops, large beads, bells, shells, tinfoil dishes, metal trays.

- Look at a variety of kitchen utensils: whisks, sugar shakers, wooden spoons and cake tins. Explore the sounds by shaking, turning, tapping them.

- Hide the utensils in a box or behind a screen, can the children identify sounds by making a tapping or scraping action with their hands?

Relevant P scale statements for Communication

P1 Pupil is willing to tolerate assistance to explore objects. They may show awareness or desire to find the source of a sound.

P2 Pupil performs some actions by trial and improvement. Pupil may repeat an activity many times, gradually improving on the outcome.

P3 Pupils explore materials in increasingly complex ways.

Watch, listen and reflect:

How does the child show growing awareness of sounds and senses?

- How do they use words, gestures, body language such as eye contact and facial expression to communicate?

- How are they developing their ability to use both hands?

- Do the pupils turn towards the stimulation source?

Activity Eight
Lip smacking good!

What does this activity help with?

Developing mouth, lip and tongue movements, which help speech.

Suitable for: 1:1

What you need:

- plastic coated spoons

- ice cubes containing mint sauce, cherry pie filling, lemon juice or fruit juice

- candy floss or melting corn snacks (Wotsits)

- honey, Marmite, syrup, ketchup or cheesy mashed potato

Note: take account of the child's likes and dislikes when working with foods.

What you do:

1. Collect together some of the suggested foods.

2. Use some of them to help children to develop their tongue and mouth movements –for example, candy floss or melting corn snacks help biting movements, honey helps with licking.

3. Offer some ice cubes containing mint sauce, cherry pie filling, lemon juice or fruit juice. (Be careful the child does not burn themselves on the ice).

4. Massage the child's cheek first, then put a smear of honey, Marmite or ketchup on their lips. This will encourage licking movements.

5. Help them to learn to close their lips to take food from a spoon by offering a spoon with a sticky substance (such as cheesy mashed potato) on it. Help them to place the spoon in their mouth the right way up and to use their top lip to remove the food.

Some more ideas:

- Imitate blowing kisses.

- Play at picking up small sweets or raisins using just their lips.

- Blow bubbles in the air or feathers along a surface.

- Try warmed substances such as chocolate, custard or thickened soup on a spoon to lick.

- Make milk lollies to lick, drink thick milk shake through straws, suck yogurt from tubes.

Relevant P scale statements for Communication

P1 Pupil moves mouth in a reflex, lip smacking movement in response to a tiny smear of substance spread on a lip.

P2 Pupil begins to move their tongue and lips intentionally.

P3 Pupil has increasing control over mouth movements and may have consistent success over some movements, such as licking, blowing, biting, moving their tongue.

Watch, listen and reflect:

How are the child's lip and mouth movements developing?

- Are mouth and lip movements increasing?

- Is tongue movement becoming more precise?

- Can they coordinate hand and mouth movements to control such foods as lollies?

- Does the child become still or more animated?

Activity Nine
Eye eye

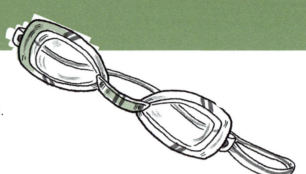

What does this activity help with?

Exploring light and vision, developing visual skills.

Suitable for: 1:1 or small group

What you need:

- mirrors

- soft toys with eyes

- photos of eyes

- safe glasses, glasses frames or sunglasses

- card and cellophane to make glasses

What you do:

1. Spend some time showing the child their own eyes in a mirror.

2. Encourage the children to look at your eyes and the eyes of other children in the group.

3. Look at a selection of soft toys and the position of their eyes.

4. Show the child an enlarged photo of an eye and look together at its different parts – the iris, pupil, eyelid, eyelash, eyebrow. Use simple language – not the technical terms!

5. Experiment with the glasses, frames and sunglasses.

6. Make card glasses with the children, letting them select their own colour of cellophane for the lenses.

7. Look at visually exciting patterns with the child – black and white, blue and yellow, red and blue.

Some more ideas:

- Visit an optician.

- Explore other types of glasses – goggles, safety glasses, swim goggles.

- Cover their eyes with a blindfold and play at guessing familiar objects. Be aware that some children hate blindfolds.

- Watch a patterned screen saver (but be aware that some children are badly affected by these repetitive patterns and they may trigger fits!).

- Make mobiles and hanging toys which turn and spin.

Relevant P scale statements for Communication

P1 Pupil moves head or eyes towards light or bright stimuli.

P2 Pupil is visually alert and may fixate on a familiar face. They may move head deliberately to see visual stimuli.

P3 Pupil visually follows direction of moving objects until object moves out of visual field. They can engage in sustained visual attention for approximately one to two minutes.

Watch, listen and reflect:

How does the child show their developing visual awareness?

- Does the child find black and white patterns or coloured patterns more interesting?

- Does the child respond to simple or complex patterns?

- Does the child avoid some activities by closing their eyes?

- Can they recognise themselves in a mirror?

Activity Ten
Sort it out

What does this activity help with?

Sorting and using tools.

Suitable for: 1:1 or small group

What you need:

- conkers and leaves

- pasta and dried peas

- flour and dry pasta

- sand and stones

- rice, salt, lentils and beans

- colanders

- sieves, strainers, bowls and spoons

What you do:

1. Collect a small amount of two types of things for the mixture (such as shells and plastic lids) and put them in two separate shallow containers. Don't have too much of anything, and match the size of the items to the child's ability and hand control. Make sure they are easy to separate again! You could start off with just a few conkers and a few leaves.

2. Look at the separate things with the children and then make mixtures of different materials which can easily be separated by hand e.g. conkers and dry leaves, pasta and peas.

3. Spend time exploring and looking at the mixtures you have made.

4. Now have a go at separating the objects out again into the two original containers. Praise their efforts at sorting, and don't go on too long.

Some more ideas:

- Make some mixtures with smaller objects such as lentils and dried peas, or sand and the paper dots from a hole punch, dried pasta and flour.

- Try a range of domestic implements for separating, e.g. sieves, tea strainers, slotted spoons, sink strainers.

- Make your own separators by punching holes in paper cups or yoghurt pots. Find out which mixtures can be separated using your home-made separator.

Relevant P scale statements for Mathematics: Number

P1 Pupil shows intolerance to a range of sensory stimuli – e.g. moves hand away from substances they find unpleasant.

P2 Pupil performs some actions using trial and error – e.g. moves hands and fingers in the mix.

P3 Pupil can explore objects and begins to repeat and control actions such as tipping a container to pour out its contents.

Watch, listen and reflect:

How does the child show their likes or dislikes of tactile experiences?

- Does the child become more animated?

- Does the child become still?

- Does the child respond to looking at themselves?

- Do they make sounds, gestures, expressions?

Activity Eleven
Exploring size

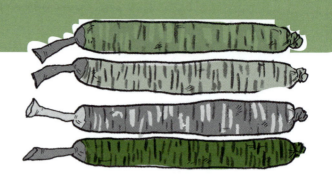

What does this activity help with?

Learning about size and shape.

Suitable for: 1:1 or small group

What you need:

- balloons

- rocket balloons (sometimes called 'Screaming Tiger Tails')

- balloon pump

What you do:

1. Let the children handle the balloons, but be vigilant and don't allow them to put them in their mouths. If you have any worries about supervision, do this activity with one child only.

2. Now put a deflated regular or rocket balloon between the child's hands. Encourage them to look at what is happening.

3. Using the balloon pump, slowly inflate the balloon saying 'Bigger, bigger, bigger and bigger' as the balloon grows. Don't over-inflate the balloon in case it bursts.

4. When the balloon is inflated talk about how big it is and give the child time to feel it, squeeze it and stroke it.

5. Remove the balloon pump and let the child hold the balloon as it deflates and buzzes. Say 'Smaller, smaller, smaller and smaller' as it shrinks.

6. Repeat with a different colour, shape or size of balloon.

Some more ideas:

- To keep children's interest, there are all sorts of balloons you can try for this activity – from little party balloons to punch bag size.

- Use a funnel to fill balloons with water (support the balloon in a shallow bowl or plant saucer to avoid accidents!).

- Hang balloons from strings so children can feel, pat and bounce them.

- Hold a balloon between you, hands on its surface, put your mouth close to the balloon and make sounds – these will vibrate the balloon.

Relevant P scale statements for Mathematics: Number

P1 Pupil responds at an early reflex level to tactile, visual and smell stimuli. May need help to participate.

P2 Pupil stretches out to hold objects using random movements. They hold objects using their whole hand and arms and let go unintentionally.

P3 Pupil uses different parts of the hand to explore objects and may let go intentionally .

Watch, listen and reflect:

How does the child show growing understanding of changing size?

- Do they respond to the changing size of the balloons?

- Do they open their hands as the balloon grows?

- Look at their facial expressions, bo children. Are they expressing likes

Activity Twelve
Let's count

What does this activity help with?

Exploring numbers and practising counting.

Suitable for: 1:1 or small group

What you need:

- box lids, plant saucers, plastic plates or other simple shallow containers

- white PVA glue

- shiny pebbles

What you do:

1. Use a small box lid, plant saucer, plastic plate or other simple shallow container. Metal dishes make a good noise!

2. Put a small number of pebbles (between 2 and 5) in another tray where each child can see and reach them. If they are unable to pick the pebbles up, make sure they can see them as you do it.

3. Depending on the child's ability and control, either:

   - let them pick up pebbles one at a time;
   - pick up pebbles and put them in their hand;
   - hold their hand and guide it to the pebbles;
   - encourage them to track your hand as you pick up pebbles.

4. If they can, encourage them to vocalise or say the numbers as you count together and drop the pebbles into the lid.

5. Repeat the activity with another number.

Some more ideas:

- If the children are at the right stage, you could add a small number card to the tray after they have added the pebbles.

- You could spread white glue on the container to stick the pebbles down for a more permanent product.

- Use shells, acorns, star anise, dry pasta shapes or conkers instead.

- Children at P7 may be able to cope with matching the number of objects to a number card you put in the lid before they start.

Relevant P scale statements for Mathematics: Number

P2(i) Pupil is willing to tolerate assistance to explore objects.

P3(i) Pupil will reach towards objects placed within their visual field and track objects as they are being counted.

P6 Pupils will put the objects into the lid as the adult counts (up to 3 objects).

P7 Pupil joins in rote counting to 10.

Watch, listen and reflect:

How does the child show their developing skills and abilities?

- Do they respond to the rhythm of counting?

- Given the opportunity, do they to say the next number in a sequence?

- Are they able to grasp and let go?

- Are they counting by eye pointing, vocalisation, words?

Activity Thirteen
Divali lights

What does this activity help with?

Responding to visual stimuli. Experiencing features of a different culture.

Suitable for: 1:1 or small group

What you need:

- sari or other Indian or Pakistani fabrics

- torches

- Indian or Pakistani music

- a Divali picture book

What you do:

1. Gather together a selection of sparkly and brightly coloured sari material, music, torches and lights of different types.

2. Play some Indian music gently in the background for this activity.

3. Explore the fabrics by feeling them, wrapping the child or yourself in them, holding them to skin on faces, arms and legs or playing peek-a-boo.

4. Shine torches onto and through the fabric, so the colours and sparkles shine. Talk about the colours and decorations.

5. You could share a Divali picture book or a story about Indian or Pakistani children.

Some more ideas:

- Dress up in woolly hats and thick scarves and go outside to shine torches in the garden.

- Wrap the children in a space blanket and shine the torch onto it.

- Get some holographic paper and shine lights onto it.

- Help the children to make some Divali lamps from clay or dough.

- Light some safe candles and watch the flames. (Never leave children alone with candles.)

Relevant P scale statements for Communication

P1   Pupil reacts to light and may turn head and eyes towards light source. They may shut their eyes when the light shines on their face.

P2(i) Pupil moves head deliberately and consistently to see visual stimuli.

P3   Pupil shows visual interest in movement with prolonged attention.

P3(ii) Pupil actively explores objects and events for periods.

Watch, listen and reflect:

How does the child show their likes or dislikes of new stimuli?

- Do they focus on the light?

- Do they follow moving lights with their eyes, or eyes and head?

- Do they enjoy being enclosed? Is this related to a schema?

- Would they enjoy other wrapping activities such as dens or tents?

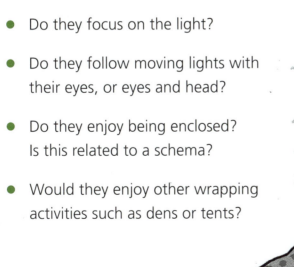

Activity Fourteen
Awesome air

What does this activity help with?

Experiencing sensory learning. Identifying and responding to moving air.

Suitable for: 1:1 or small group

What you need:

- fans, hairdryer, 'Airzooka'

- light items for flapping games

- straws

- squeezy bottles or light skittles

- table-tennis balls, balloons

- plastic bubbles or magic bubbles, streamers and feathers

What you do:

1. Show the child how they can make air move using fans, hair dryers, an 'Airzooka' (see below), or by flapping a sheet.

2. Play at blowing light objects such as bubbles, tissue paper, feathers and streamers.

3. Show the child how to make sounds by exhaling vigorously, or blowing through their pursed lips. Feel their own rib cages move as they breath in and out. Listen to and copy different breathing sounds – snoring, coughing, gasping, sniffing, panting and sucking in.

4. Squeeze clean, empty squeezy bottles to feel the air coming out.

5. Blow bubbles and balloons. Use straws to move light items across a table or the floor.

6. Blow the surface of liquids in bowls and cups. Use straws to make bubble pictures or froth in milk.

Some more ideas:

- Go outside to feel the air on skin and hair. It doesn't need to be very windy – try wetting hands or cheeks so you can feel the breeze on a calm day.

- Play with bubbles on a windy day – get a bubble machine and chase the bubbles in the garden.

- Fly small wind socks, windmills, flags and streamers. Make bunting from triangles or squares of fabric stapled to string.

Relevant P scale statements for Communication

P1 Pupil shows simple reflex response to a sudden unfamiliar event e.g. startles when blown on. (Science)

P2 Pupil begins to show an interest in people and events e.g. focusing on sensory aspects of stories and rhymes.

P3 Pupil explores experiences in increasingly complex ways e.g. reaches towards objects moving in the air.

Watch, listen and reflect:

How does the child show their responses to moving air?

- Does the child become more animated or more still?

- How do they respond to different tactile experiences?

- Watch for children reaching towards objects as they are blown and tracking them as they move.

Activity Fifteen
Magic mixtures

What does this activity help with?

Using the senses as children experience changing materials.

Suitable for: a small group

What you need:

- a large bucket for a cauldron

- a selection of fresh herbs – sage, mint, rosemary, lemon balm, basil, tarragon, bay leaves etcj

- any other natural materials e.g. large pebbles, twigs, leaves, flowers, pine cones, conkers etc

- warm water in a watering can or jug

- a stick for stirring

What you do:

1. Take the children into your outdoor area or garden (or the local park) and collect some ingredients to add to your potion. Talk about them with the children. Ask what they think will happen if they mix the things together to make potions or magic mixtures. (Emphasise that potions are not to drink!)

2. Place them in the bucket and stir them with the stick. Make sure all the children have a go. Look at what is happening.

3. Now show them the herbs you have brought. Explore the smell of the different herbs as the children help to rip the leaves and add them to the potion. Keep watching and talking.

4. Help the children to pour some warm water onto the mixture. Warm water will help to release the smells and perfumes of your mixture.

5. Talk about the aroma of the potion as you stir.

Some more ideas:

- Take photos of the activity at different stages and make a display or a photo book. If you import the photos into PowerPoint, the children can watch it themselves.

- Put individual potions into jars labelled with the children's names.

- Experiment with other mixtures – flour and water, shaving foam and food colouring, dry sand and water, sugar and water, pasta cooked with food colouring. Talk about what happens when things are mixed.

Relevant P scale statements for Communication

P2(i)   Pupil reacts to new activities.

P3   Pupil observes the results of their own actions. They actively explore objects and events for more extended periods. (Science)

P4   Pupil explores objects and materials provided, changing some materials by physical means and observing outcomes. (Science)

Watch, listen and reflect:

How does the child show their likes or dislikes of new activities?

- Can they grasp items and release them into the container?

- Can children collect and make their own mixtures?

- Try to make non-judgmental, positive responses to things that children like/dislike.

Activity Sixteen
All kinds of weather

What does this activity help with?

Responding to sensory experiences, experiencing different weathers.

Suitable for: Small or larger group

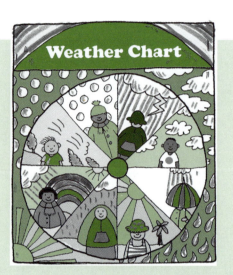

What you need:

- pictures of different weather conditions
- wheat bag (See resources)
- a selection of percussion instruments
- a fan
- dry leaves
- plastic bottles and string
- a water spray
- an umbrella
- rice, pasta and dried beans
- plastic tray

What you do:

Emphasise the weather by simple sensory experiences:

- In sunny weather, look at pictures of sunny day activities, talk to the child about feeling warm in the sun. Give the child a heated wheat bag to feel warmth. Create quiet warm weather sounds with metal wind chimes, Indian bells and triangles. Add sound effects e.g. birds, running water, sea.

- In windy weather look at pictures of kites and leaves blowing in the wind. Feel the wind, blow onto the child and use card fans or electrical fans. Create wind sounds with whirly tubes, wooden wind chimes, rattles, dry leaves. Blow objects such as suspended plastic bottles with a fan to make sounds.

- In rainy weather look at pictures of a rainy day. Listen to rain dripping from a water spray onto a large umbrella. Create rain sounds by patting knees, tapping feet, pouring rice, pasta or beans onto a plastic tray. Play a rain-stick or shakers.

- In snowy or frosty weather look at pictures of snow and ice. Make frosty sounds with bells and other metal objects. Feel ice cubes, watch snow melt.

Some more ideas:

- Go outside whenever you can so children get used to all the different sorts of weather.

- Collect stories where weather features.

- Make weather bags for outside play – ribbon sticks and kites for windy days, umbrellas, boots and rain hats for wet days, sun hats and sunglasses for sunny days etc.

- Make a simple weather chart and talk about the weather every day.

Relevant P scale statements for Communication

P2(i)   Pupil shows emerging awareness of experiences and activities.

P2(i)   Pupil reacts to new activities and experiences.

P2(ii) Pupil cooperates with shared exploration and supported participation. (Science)

P6   Pupil closely observes changes that occur in such features as food and weather.

Watch, listen and reflect:

How does the child show their likes or dislikes of different weathers?

- Do they welcome the opportunity to respond to what they see, hear, taste, touch and smell?

- Can you see facial expressions, body language and other responses made by children?

- Can they tell the difference between different weathers?

Activity Seventeen
Party pakora

What does this activity help with?

Responding to sensory stimuli. Experiencing features of a different culture.

Suitable for: 1:1 or a small group

What you need:

- aprons
- clean hands
- bowls, spoons
- prepared vegetables
- raw potato, onion, spinach and ginger
- gram flour (an Asian flour made from chick peas)
- methi (a leafy herb you can get from an Asian grocer)
- spices – garam masala, salt

The ingredients can be adjusted to taste or according to what you have. Try peas, beans, carrots, swede etc.

What you do:

Decide whether the children will be able to concentrate for the whole of this activity. If not, prepare some of the ingredients in advance. This could include chopping the vegetables into small dice, mixing them and frying some pakora in advance.

1. Explore the raw vegetables you are going to use with the children. Allow the child time to feel, smell, look, and taste – or show the children the previously chopped vegetables, letting them touch and taste things if they want to.

2. Let the children smell the spices and then add them to the bowl.

3. Give the child some gram flour in a bowl to explore.

4. Add gram flour to the pakora mix until everything is coated and the mixture holds together (you may need to add a bit of water).

5. Smell, explore and taste previously fried pakora, or let them watch from a safe distance as you cook the ones they have made.

Some more ideas:

- Vary the vegetables. Try cauliflower, broccoli, aubergine, tomatoes, courgettes, okra, peas.

- Make some samosas using cooked vegetables wrapped in thinly rolled pastry and fried. The good thing about these is that it doesn't matter if the wrapping is a bit untidy!

- Make pakoras or chappatis (from 2 cups flour, 1 tablespoon oil, and water to mix). Roll out into rounds and fry in a little oil. Eat with yogurt.

Relevant P scale statements for Communication

P1 Pupil responds at an early reflex level to tactile visual, smell and taste stimuli. They may need help to participate.

P2 Pupil communicates simple like and dislike through vocalisation and gesture.

P3 Pupil able to make choices and will request preferred items by vocalising or gesturing to them.

Watch, listen and reflect:

How does the child show their likes or dislikes of new foods?

- How do they respond to what they see touch, smell and taste?

- Note facial expressions, body language and other responses.

- How do they respond to trying new tastes and flavours?

Activity Eighteen
Take off!

What does this activity help with?
Using ICT to enhance learning through topics.

Suitable for: 1:1 or a small group

What you need:

- video, photos or books about rockets and space
- microphone
- echo mike
- tape recorder
- a camera
- collage materials
- glue

What you do:

1. Look at some pictures, books or video about space.

2. Practise counting down from 10 together as you watch rockets take off. (Google some images of space rockets or look at the NASA website.)

3. Make some rockets from recycled materials, then make some space and rocket sounds into a microphone and amplify them to play back. Or use an echo mike to make your voices into alien voices. Play your sounds back, as you fly the rockets into space.

4. Use a simple computer paint program to draw over photos of the children and turn them into spacemen.

5. Or use photos of the children and change them by adding collage materials e.g. make a body out of stainless steel scouring sponges, foil or other shiny materials.

Relevant P scale statements for ICT

P1   Pupil shows emerging awareness of activities and experiences. They may give intermittent reactions e.g. to lights, sounds etc.

P2   Pupil begins to show interest in people, events and objects, e.g. tracking movement across a TV screen.

P3(iii) Pupil actively explores objects and events for more extended periods.

Watch, listen and reflect:

How does the child show their involvement in the project?

- Do they create sounds spontaneously?

- Do they experiment with sounds and sound makers?

- Do they make choices when using collage or construction materials?

- How is their use of ICT developing?

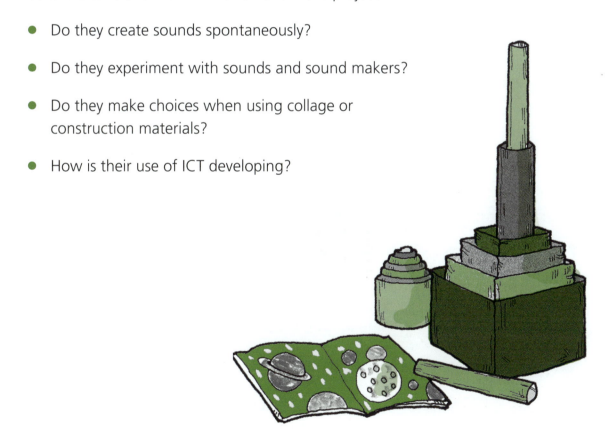

Activity Nineteen
Fruity colours

What does this activity help with?

Experiencing, identifying and naming colours through sensory activities.

Suitable for: 1:1 or a small group

What you need:

- some round shaped fruit – an orange, an apple, a lemon, a lime, a beef tomato, (whatever you can get)

- balls to paint

- red, orange, green and yellow paint (to match the fruits you have chosen)

What you do:

1. Start by looking at and handling the fruit. Adjust the number of different fruits in a session to the developmental stage of the children.
   Remember that you will probably get a better reaction with two or three.

2. Now offer some sensory experiences using the different fruit:

   - put an orange in a warm place before feeling and smelling it

   - scrape the skin of a lemon so you can smell the citrus oil

   - polish a shiny apple to look at and touch

   - put a finger on a cut lime to taste the sharp juice

   - cut a beef tomato in half and look inside.

2. Now look at the paints you have chosen. Talk about which paint matches which fruit, tip some of the colours into shallow containers and let the children roll the balls until they are covered in paint. When dry, use the balls to make a colour mobile.

Some more ideas:

- Try exploring long thin fruit and vegetables such as bananas, cucumbers, courgettes, leeks or runner beans and using cardboard tubes to make the mobile.

- Look at fruit with more subtle colours (purple plums and aubergines; orange carrots and apricots; yellow pears and starfruit).

- Explore textured fruit such as pineapples and fuzzy peaches, or berries – strawberries, raspberries, blueberries, cranberries.

Relevant P scale statements for Communication

P1   Pupil responds at an early reflex level to tactile visual, smell and taste stimuli. You may have to help them to participate.

P2   Pupil stretches out to grasp objects using random movements. They hold objects using their whole hand and let go unintentionally.

P3   Pupil uses different parts of the hand to explore the fruit and to paint the balls.

Watch, listen and reflect:

How does the child show their likes or dislikes of their new foods and textures?

- Does the child become more animated?

- Does the child become still?

- Does the child respond to looking at themselves?

- Do they make sounds, gestures, expressions?

Activity Twenty
Edible artwork

What does this activity help with?

(choose sweet or savoury biscuits according to the preference of the children or your setting's healthy eating guidance)

Suitable for: 1:1 or a small group

What you need:

- plain biscuits (sweet or savoury)
- boards or plates
- piping icing or cream cheese in a tube
- aprons
- clean hands

What you do:

1. Look at the tubes of icing/cheese and talk about how they work. Demonstrate how to use them by squeezing a bit on a plate. Don't be tempted to draw a picture, this may inhibit children's creativity.

2. Let the children feel the texture and taste a little of the cheese or icing. Talk about different colours if you have more than one.

3. Unpack the biscuits and put one on a plate for each child.

4. Help them to decorate their own biscuit. Some children may be able to do this unaided, some may need your hand over theirs, some may need to watch you. Let them be as independent as possible.

5. Take some photos before the biscuits are eaten!

Some more ideas:

- More able children, or those who have done this activity before may like to add cake decorations to sweet biscuits or chopped tomato and herbs to savoury ones. You could use tomato ketchup or Marmite squeezy bottles for different flavours and colours.

- Try making faces, flowers or shapes with the decorations.

- Make your own biscuits from a simple recipe and add decorations. Don't forget that some children find it impossible to resist eating them!

Relevant P scale statements for Communication

P1 Pupil responds at an early reflex level to tactile visual, smell and taste stimuli. You may have to help them.

P2 Pupil stretches out to grasp objects using random movements. They hold objects using their whole hand and let go unintentionally.

P3 Pupil uses inferior pincer grip (thumb and index finger but not finger tip).

Watch, listen and reflect:

How do the children show their physical and creative skills in this activity?

- Can they squeeze the tubes unaided?

- Do they show excitement?

- How long can they concentrate?

- Do they make sounds, gestures, or other movements as they work?

Activity Twenty One
A weaving wheel

What does this activity help with?
Exploring texture, colour and shape.

Suitable for: a small group

What you need:

- an old bicycle wheel (ask your local bike shop)

- a variety of different colours and textures of materials cut into strips

What you do:

1. Try to get the widest possible range of fabrics including leather, fur, fleece, glitter, sequin waste, tinsel etc.

2. Sit with the children and explore the different colours and textures of the strips of fabric. Talk about them, using descriptive words such as fluffy, smooth, shiny, bright, pattern. Stroke the fabrics on hands and arms, noting children's responses.

3. Now show the children the bike wheel and talk about what it is.

4. Let the children help you to tie and weave the strips of fabric in and out of the spokes of the wheel to make a collaborative weaving. Don't worry if the children can't tie or weave accurately – the important thing is for them to work as independently as possible.

5. Support children who are finding the task difficult by holding their hands or showing them how to push the strips through the spokes.

Some more ideas:

- Use different structures for tying and weaving – oven shelves or cooling racks, plastic covered garden fence, trellis, netting or the fence in the garden.

- Make seasonal or topic inspired weavings and hangings by using different colours and adding natural objects: browns and oranges with added leaves for Autumn or flowers in Spring; blues and greens with cellophane, shells and fish for a seaside hanging; silver, white and blue for a frosty winter or Christmas weaving.

Relevant P scale statements for Communication

P1(ii) Pupil can grasp objects briefly when placed in their hand, where finger gripping is an instinctive reflex. Pupils' limbs may be active but movement is gross and uncontrolled.

P3 Pupil's actions are more deliberate and when reaching out towards an object the index finger may be extended. They actively explore objects and materials.

Watch, listen and reflect:

How does the child demonstrate their growing ability and independence?

- How are arm and finger movements developing as you assist them?

- Do they look at what they are doing?

- How are they responding to tactile and visual qualities of materials and selecting those they like?

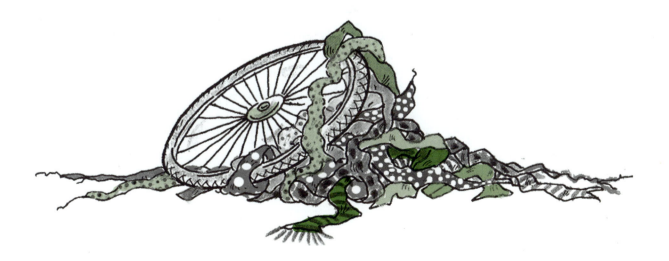

Activity Twenty Two
Fruity faces

What does this activity help with?

Using sensory experiences to develop choice and creativity.

Suitable for: 1:1 or a small group

What you need:

- pieces of fruit in individual bowls, some whole, some cut

- paper plates

- aprons, clean hands

- a camera

What you do:

1. You could prepare some fruity faces before the session and take photos to show the children, or find some in children's cook books or books on healthy eating.

2. Show the children the different sorts of fruit you have prepared. You may want to let them taste some – they will want to!

3. Now show them some pictures of fruity faces or make a simple one yourself (the danger is they will all make the same one, so be cautious!).

4. Now give each child a paper plate and let them make their own fruity faces. Take photos during the activity so you can note their reactions.

5. Give plenty of praise, even when you have helped. This will ensure their continuing attention.

6. Photograph the completed creations before they are eaten.

Some more ideas:

- Make other food creations for snack or lunchtimes. They will often tempt reluctant eaters.

- Make vegetable creatures or minibeasts from raw vegetables and fruit.

- Use mashed potato, sweet potato or mashed swede as an alternative for messy play or mark making.

- Print with cut fruit or vegetables such as carrots, potatoes, oranges, apples. Stick a fork securely in the pieces to make them easier to hold.

Relevant P scale statements for Communication

P1   Pupil responds at an early reflex level to tactile visual, smell and taste stimuli. You may have to help them to participate.

P2   Pupil stretches out to grasp objects using random movements. They hold objects using their whole hand and let go unintentionally.

P3   Pupil uses inferior pincer grip (thumb and index finger but not finger tip).

Watch, listen and reflect:

How does the child show their control and creativity?

- Do they respond with more than one sense?

- Do they become agitated and excited?

- Can they select items without help and arrange them on the plate?

- Can they wait to eat it till they have finished the face?

Activity Twenty Three
Jelly wobble

What does this activity help with?

Sensory experiences with hands and feet, exploring malleable materials.

Suitable for: 1:1

What you need:

- jelly

- small unbreakable mirrors the size of small trays

- soapy water and towels to wash the children's hands and feet after the activity

What you do:

This activity needs careful supervision to avoid slipping on the mirrors. Provide individual trays to prevent possible infection.

1. Make a large quantity of jelly (all one colour and flavour works best).

2. Tip some of the jelly onto individual mirrors.

3. Give the children plenty of time to explore the jelly, using either their hands or bare feet.

4. Play alongside and let them smell, feel, taste and look at the jelly. Talk about the texture, smell and colour as they play.

5. Support children who want to stand – it will be slippery!

6. Follow the child's lead as they play, and be ready to stop when they have had enough.

7. Use plenty of warm soapy water to clean away the jelly when they have finished. This can provide another pleasant sensory experience.

Some more ideas:

- Try some different ideas for malleable experiences. How about these?
    Stuffing – herby ones are best for sensory experiences
    Thick porridge with orange zest or flavouring added
    Dried fruit soaked overnight in cold tea
    Cranberries and red cabbage (raw or cooked).

- Children who are resistant to tactile experiences may find feeling with feet easier.

- Some children respond better to warm experiences than cold ones!

Relevant P scale statements for Communication

P1(i)   Pupil shows intolerance or tolerance to a range of sensory stimuli.

P2   Pupil interacts with stimuli by reaching for and holding them. They may use a smearing action.

P3   Pupil can explore and interact with stimuli spontaneously. They may use hand and finger movements to explore stimuli.

Watch, listen and reflect:

How does the child show their likes or dislikes in this activity?

- Do they look at what they are doing?

- Can you tell if they like it?

- Do they notice the mirror?

- How do you know if they like it?

- Do they enjoy washing after the activity?

Activity Twenty Four
Toppling towers

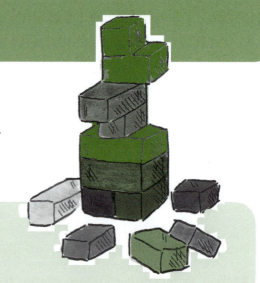

What does this activity help with?
Developing whole arm and manual dexterity and control.

Suitable for: a small group

What you need:

- empty boxes of all sorts, sizes and shapes

What you do:
This is a game of building, balance and 'one more', not a sticking activity.

1. Collect a range of big and middle sized boxes of all sorts of shapes.

2. Work with the child, helping them if they need it, to build towers of boxes. Each time you add one, say 'One more'.

3. When your tower is complete say 'Ready, steady, push!' as you encourage the child to push it over.

4. React when the tower falls to add fun to the game. You may have to exaggerate the surprise to make the point!

5. Continue the game for as long as the child is enjoying it – this may be a long time! You can vary the boxes you offer as the game continues.

Some more ideas:

- Collect some smaller boxes for more careful stacking, or for children who need to work at a table.

- Work with a small group, taking turns to stack the boxes to encourage working together.

- Play the turn taking game with wooden blocks, bricks or stacking beakers.

- Use big cartons outside for a bigger game, or buy a giant Jenga Game.

Relevant P scale statements for Communication

P1   Pupil is willing to explore objects and can grasp objects briefly when placed in their hand.

P2   Pupil can make a small movement to accept a small item and hold arms wide to accept a large item.

P3   Pupil can grasp two shapes at once and explore whether or not they fit together e.g. they put one box on top of another.

Watch, listen and reflect:

How does the child show their ability and enjoyment in the activity?

- How are their arm muscles developing as they push towers over?

- Are they looking at what they are doing?

- Do they copy what you are saying or counting?

- Do they choose the next box or pick it randomly?

Activity Twenty Five
Tiny things

What does this activity help with?
Developing fine motor skills in hand and finger movements.

Suitable for: 1:1 and small groups

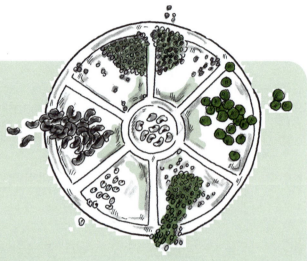

What you need:
- a variety of small containers, spoons, scoops and funnels

- dry wild or basmati rice,

- red, green and yellow lentils

- mung or aduki beans

- spice seeds e.g. cumin, fennel, cinnamon stick

- dry tea leaves

What you do:

1. Set up a tuffspot or large tray with lots of small, lightweight dried foods – no tools at this stage.

2. Explore the objects without tools first – poking, scooping and pouring with fingers and hands. Some children may need to be encouraged and you may have to model movements. Don't worry if the ingredients get mixed up, it's the sensory experience that's important.

3. Give plenty of time to explore before saying anything, just play alongside, watching and listening. When the child is ready, join in by talking as you play together.

4. For some children this may be enough. If they are happy just feeling and using their hands, don't hurry to add scoops, spoons or containers. Just wait for another time.

Some more ideas:

- Add some simple tools and, if needed, model tipping, pouring, grasping, transferring and using the tools. Try simple spoons and scoops at first, then add containers, funnels, boxes and small plastic bags.

- Add herbs and spices to give the mix a different smell.

- Try coffee beans on a yellow tray (yellow will provide a good visual contrast), black beans on a white tray, or white beans on a red tray.

Relevant P scale statements for Communication

P1   Pupil can grip object placed in hand where finger gripping is an instinctive reflex. Pupil's limbs may be active but movement is gross and uncontrolled.

P2   Pupil can release object by dropping but may not yet be able to place an object on a surface voluntarily.

P3   Pupil's actions are more deliberate and when reaching out towards an object the index finger may be extended.

Watch, listen and reflect:

How does the child show their growing control of hands and fingers?

- Do individual children like having their hands in the mixture of tiny things?

- Do they explore and transfer the mixture with their hands and fingers?

- Can the child use tools to transfer the mixture into and out of containers?

Key contacts, resources and websites

More information on the P levels and their use
qca.org.uk or www.standards.dfes.gov.uk

B Squared
Burnhill Business Centre Provident House
Burrell Row, High Street, Beckenham,
Kent, BR3 1AT
info@bsquaredsen.co.uk

Equals Schemes of Work
EQUALS PO Box 107 North Shields
Tyne and Wear NE30 2YG
www.equals.co.uk

Literacy for Very Special People
ISBN 1900231506
by Flo Longhorn
Catalyst Education Resources Ltd

EYFS Framework
DfES Publications
PO Box 5050 Sherwood Park Annesley
Nottingham NG15 ODJ
ref: 00012-2007PCK-EN
ISBN: 978-1-84478-886-6

Early Years Support Team
based at: RNI for Deaf People,
19-23 Featherstone St London EC1Y 8SL
www.earlysupport.org.uk

The Staff of Ivy House Special School
(whose work inspired this book)
Moorway Lane
Littleover
Derby DE23 2FS
01332 344694

Little Baby Books and Little Books
A&C Black
36 Soho Square
London W1D 3QY
www.acblack.com/featherstone

The Small World Recipe Book
Helen Bromley
Lawrence Educational Publications
17 Redruth Rd
Walsall
West Midlands

PIVATS
Lancashire County Council
e-mail lpds.marketing@ed.lancscc.gov.uk

Finger toothbrush and gum massager
Baby Eden
www.babyeden.co.uk

Glycerine mouth swabs
Medisave
www.medisave.co.uk

Airzooka
Hawkin's Bazaar
www.hawkin.com

Wheat bags
Mobility Aids UK
www.mobilityaidsuk.co.uk